GREAT ZOOS OF THE UNITED STATES ™

SAN ANTONIO ZOO

STACY McREYNOLDS

The Rosen Publishing Group's
PowerKids Press ™
New York

Dedicated to Frick and Frack and nature lovers across the world

 A message to Rosen readers from the San Antonio Zoo:

Our vision is to become one of the nation's premier zoos which promotes conservation through education. It is the mission of the San Antonio Zoological Gardens and Aquarium to foster appreciation and concern for all living things. We are dedicated to providing: the highest standard of care for our animal and plant collection; a diverse educational and high quality recreational experience for all visitors; all the resources at our disposal for the conservation of the Earth's flora and fauna.

Published in 2003 by The Rosen Publishing Group, Inc.
29 East 21st Street, New York, NY 10010

First Edition

Editor: Natashya Wilson
Book Design: Michael J. Caroleo and Michael de Guzman

Photo Credits: Cover, title page, pp. 4, 7 (inset left), 11 (top, center), 15 Maura B. McConnell; p. 8 © Mark Langford; pp. 8 (inset top), 16 (bottom) © Patricia M. McGrath; p. 16 (top left) Mark Mayfield; pp. 7 (map), 8 (logo), and all other photos courtesy of the San Antonio Zoo.

McReynolds, Stacy.
    San Antonio Zoo / Stacy McReynolds.
        p. cm. — (Great zoos of the United States)
    Summary: An inside look at the San Antonio Zoo, focusing mainly on its operation and its conservation efforts.
    Includes bibliographical references (p.   ).
    ISBN 0-8239-6319-5 (lib. bdg.)
    1. San Antonio Zoological Gardens & Aquarium—Juvenile literature. [1. San Antonio Zoological Gardens & Aquarium.
    2. Zoos.] I. Title. II. Series.
    QL76.5.U62 S2596 2003
    590'.7'3764351—dc21

                    2002000159

Manufactured in the United States of America

CONTENTS

1 A Rocky Beginning   5

2 Many Animals, Many Needs   6

3 Working Together to Save the World   9

4 What's for Dinner?   10

5 What the Zoo Doctor Ordered   13

6 Safety First   14

7 Zoo Babies   17

8 Planes, Trains, and Automobiles   18

9 Hope for Whooping Cranes   21

10 A Living Classroom   22

Glossary   23

Index   24

Web Sites   24

The rock walls of the former limestone quarry now form natural fences for the homes of many Zoo animals, such as this lion.

A Rocky Beginning

As you walk through San Antonio Zoo in Texas, you will see steep rock walls. This is because the Zoo is located in an old limestone **quarry**. Early San Antonio settlers used rocks from this site to build houses, churches, and even the **Alamo**. Around 1914, Colonel George W. Brackenridge placed animals in the quarry, in Brackenridge Park. San Antonio Zoo began with these bears, buffalo, deer, elk, lions, and monkeys. During the **Great Depression**, hundreds of workers from the **Works Progress Administration** helped to build the Zoo. Known for its exhibits without bars and its **conservation** and education programs, the San Antonio Zoo has become one of the United States's top zoos.

MANY ANIMALS, MANY NEEDS

The San Antonio Zoo keeps more than 750 different **species** of animals from around the world. Caring for the animals and running the Zoo is a full-time job for 150 workers and 200 **volunteers**. The Zoo is **nonprofit**, so most of its $10-million-per-year **budget** comes from money spent by visitors to the Zoo.

Zoo animals need food, water, shelter, and space. Each exhibit is specially made for the animals that live in it. To make the animals comfortable and to show how animals live in the wild, the Zoo makes the exhibits as natural as possible. Many exhibits feature plants from the animals' native lands, and many house more than one kind of animal.

Zoo maps guide visitors around the Zoo's 52 acres (21 ha). The San Antonio River supplies plenty of water for the animals.

The Zoo's gibbons have many branches to swing from in their home. They use their long arms to move from branch to branch.

Aza is the official spokescritter of the
AMERICAN ZOO AND AQUARIUM ASSOCIATION

The AZA's official logo

WORKING TOGETHER TO SAVE THE WORLD

Zoos are more than just places to see wild animals up close. They manage many projects that help to save wild animals and wild places. With more than 200 members, the American Zoo and Aquarium Association (AZA) is active in **research**, conservation, and education. As one of the first four AZA members, the San Antonio Zoo has long been a leader in the zoo world. Some of the Zoo's projects include helping to study zebras in Kenya, Africa, and helping to save the wildlife of Madagascar. The Zoo also works with the governments of several countries to protect animal habitats and to **breed** animals to be **released** into the wild. These animals include the whooping crane and the Virgin Island boa.

WHAT'S FOR DINNER?

Can you imagine cooking for more than 3,500 people? The Zoo's **Nutrition** Center makes meals for that many animals every day. The Zoo goes through 64,000 pounds (29,030 kg) of meat, 15,000 pounds (6,804 kg) of fish, 102,000 pounds (46,266 kg) of fruits and vegetables, 8,500 bales of hay, and nearly 500,000 crickets every year!

To keep the animals active, the Zoo provides them with **enrichment**. Keepers move the animals' food so that the animals have to work to find it. They give the animals toys, change their **diets**, and rub interesting smells in their exhibits. Enrichment makes the animals think and gives them something interesting to do each day.

DID YOU KNOW?

The reticulated python is the world's longest snake. A reticulated python can grow to be 33 feet (10 m) long!

To keep the animals healthy, the Zoo feeds them restaurant-quality foods. Each animal has a special diet.

On hot days, the Zoo makes popsicles for many of the animals by freezing the animals' favorite foods in water.

The Zoo's reticulated python eats once every three months. It is more than 25 feet (7.5 m) long.

11

Daily activities such as trimming the elephants' feet and filing the hippos' tusks help to keep Zoo animals healthy.

WHAT THE ZOO DOCTOR ORDERED

From a lumpy snake to a wheezing monkey to a bird that just won't eat, zoo doctors, called veterinarians, never know what kind of animal they may be treating from one day to the next. The San Antonio Zoo has two vets and other special staff who take care of the more than 3,500 animals. These vets rely on the zookeepers to tell them when animals are not feeling well. Getting close enough to treat an animal can be very hard. San Antonio zookeepers train the animals to stand still for the vets while they give shots or take blood. Keepers have trained elephants to pick up their feet and to stretch out their ears for check-ups. Rhinos are trained to move into safety chutes to have their teeth brushed.

SAFETY FIRST

Can you imagine cleaning a cobra's home or feeding a grizzly bear? San Antonio zookeepers do these kinds of things every day. Animals at the Zoo are still wild, so keepers have to be extra careful when they take care of them. Animals such as lions, rhinos, bears, and elephants always have safety fences between them and their keepers. When it is time to clean the exhibits, keepers use food to move the animals into separate areas. Once the animals are locked away, keepers can enter the exhibits. Keepers use long, metal hooks to move **venomous** snakes from one place to another. For safety the Zoo keeps **antivenin**, a special medicine for snakebites, on hand in case a person gets bitten.

Top: *Safety fences protect both animals and people.*
Bottom: *Special hooks are used to move dangerous snakes safely.*

The Zoo produced the first white rhino (top right) born in North America and was the first zoo to raise Caribbean flamingos (top left).

The Zoo is known worldwide for its success in breeding snow leopards.

Zoo babies are cute and fun to watch. They are also a lot of work! The Zoo tries to keep babies and moms together in the exhibits. Zookeepers check on babies often, to make sure that their mothers are caring for them and that they are getting along with the other animals in their group. Vets also check on the babies often.

Many zoos are helping to save **endangered** animals by working together through programs called **Species Survival Plans** (SSPs). SSPs pick out the best possible parents. Then zoos loan animals to one another for breeding. This gives the babies the best possible chance for survival. A few of these babies may be placed into the wild when they are grown.

17

Planes, Trains, and Automobiles

As the San Antonio Zoo's babies get older, often they are moved to other zoos. Shipping animals can be interesting. When the Zoo shipped a koala to California, the koala traveled first class! The koala and its keeper each had a first-class seat on the airplane. Safe in its crate, the koala spent the entire flight sleeping. Most animals that travel do not need a keeper with them on the plane. Many animals are shipped in trailers. Some birds and reptiles go by overnight mail. When a new animal comes to the Zoo, it is kept separate from the other animals for at least 30 days. This gives the vets time to make sure the new animal is healthy and won't make the other Zoo animals sick.

Some animals travel in wooden or metal crates. The kangaroo (bottom right) *traveled to another zoo in a wooden crate (top).*

As of 2001, San Antonio Zoo is the only U.S. zoo that breeds whooping cranes.

Crockett's keeper fed her by hand using a puppet that looks like an adult whooping crane.

Whooping cranes are the tallest birds in North America. An adult male can stand 5 feet (1.5 m) tall.

Hope for Whooping Cranes

In the 1940s, there were fewer than 20 whooping cranes left in the world. Today, with help from the San Antonio Zoo, there are more than 400 whooping cranes! Crockett is a whooping crane that hatched at the Zoo on March 12, 1999. She was raised by two keepers, but she didn't know it. Keepers wear costumes and feed the chicks with a special puppet that looks like an adult crane. This keeps the chicks from getting used to seeing people. Crockett and another bird, Bowie, were the first whooping cranes from the Zoo to be placed in the wild. Before their release, the birds had to learn to find food, to fly, and where to sleep. After six months of learning, Crockett and Bowie were set free in Florida.

A Living Classroom

Did you know that the San Antonio Zoo is actually a huge classroom? One important job of the Zoo is to teach people about animals and nature. Visitors can learn a lot just by walking through the Zoo. Staff and volunteers love to answer questions. To learn more, visitors can sign up for special programs. There are behind-the-scenes tours, overnight stays, summer camps, school presentations, family programs, and more! The Zoo even hosts trips to other countries, such as Africa and Costa Rica. Another great way to learn about animals at the Zoo is to join a volunteer program. By teaching people to care about animals, the Zoo helps to protect wild animals and the places where they live.

Glossary

Alamo (A-luh-moh) A place called a mission where a famous battle was fought during the Texas Revolution.

antivenin (an-tih-VEH-nuhn) A medicine used to treat snakebites.

breed (BREED) To bring animals together to have babies.

budget (BUH jit) A plan for how money should be spent.

conservation (kon-sur-VAY-shun) Work done to save wild animals and their homes.

diets (DY-uts) Foods animals normally eat.

endangered (en-DAYN-jerd) In danger of dying out within 20 years.

enrichment (in-RICH-mint) Objects and activities that keep animals busy and make them think.

Great Depression (GRAYT dih-PREH-shun) A time in the 1930s when banks and businesses lost money and many people lost their jobs.

nonprofit (non-PRAH-fit) Not run to make money.

nutrition (noo-TRIH-shun) Foods needed to stay healthy.

quarry (KWAHR-ee) A big hole dug to take stone from the ground.

released (ree-LEESD) Put back into, let go.

research (REE-serch) To study something carefully to find out more about it.

species (SPEE-sheez) A single kind of plant or animal.

Species Survival Plans (SPEE-sheez sur-VY-vul PLANZ) Programs that bring certain male and female animals together to make the healthiest babies so that endangered animals will not die out.

venomous (VEH-nuh-mis) Having a bite that can make other animals sick.

volunteers (vah-lun-TEERZ) People who offer to work for no pay.

Works Progress Administration (WERKS PRAH-gres ad-mih-nuh-STRAY-shun) A 1930s government project that gave people with no jobs work building parks and roads.

INDEX

A
Alamo, 5
American Zoo and
    Aquarium
    Association
    (AZA), 9
antivenin, 14

B
Bowie, 21
Brackenridge,
    Colonel George
    W., 5
breed(ing), 9, 17

C
Costa Rica, 22
Crockett, 21

E
elephants, 13–14
endangered, 17
enrichment, 10

G
Great Depression, 5

K
koala, 18

N
Nutrition Center, 10

S
Species Survival
    Plans (SSPs), 17

V
veterinarians, 13,
    17–18
volunteers, 6, 22

W
whooping cranes,
    21
Works Progress
    Administration, 5

WEB SITES

Due to the changing nature of Internet links, PowerKids Press has developed an online list of Web sites related to the subject of this book. This site is updated regularly. Please use this link to access the list:

www.powerkidslinks.com/gzus/sanantoz/